Ripley's Believe It or Not!

Baseball Oddities & Trivia

BALL TWO

by TIM O'BRIEN • • • illustrations by JOHN GRAZIANO

In Memoriam

LAWRENCE "YOGI" BERRA PASSED AWAY ON SEPTEMBER 22ND, 2015, THE 69TH ANNIVERSARY OF HIS MAJOR LEAGUE BASEBALL® DEBUT.

A Salute to Yogi on pages 36-38

Ripley's Believe It or Not! Baseball Oddities & Trivia – Ball Two!

Copyright © 2016 by Ripley Entertainment Inc. Printed and bound in Nashville, TN, U.S.A. All rights reserved. No part of this book may be reproduced or transmitted in any form or by any means, electronic or mechanical, without prior written permission from the author. Reviewers may quote brief passages in a review to be printed in a magazine, newspaper, or on the Web without written permission.

First printing
ISBN: 978-1-60991-171-3
Library of Congress Control Number (LCCN): 2015960695

Compiled, written, and edited: Tim O'Brien
Illustrations: John Graziano
Cover: John Graziano and Jennifer Wright
Page and text design: Jennifer Wright
Distribution: Ingram Global Publisher Services

This book can be customized and sold in bulk for special promotional purposes. Contact Tim O'Brien at tim@casaflamingo.com for details.

For additional copies of *Ripley's Believe It or Not! Baseball Oddities & Trivia – Ball Two!* ask your local bookseller to order it for you or visit www.amazon.com.

••• Introduction •••

To those who have been asking for more outrageous baseball factoids. Here it is! Your journey through the weird, wacky and absolutely true world of America's favorite pastime now continues! Welcome to our second volume of baseball oddities and trivia. As Yogi Berra would say, "It's like déjà vu all over again."

Our first volume, published in 2008 was a run-away hit and over the years, I have been asked many times if a second volume was in the making. This year, with Ripley's first-ever all-baseball exhibit at the Louisville Slugger Museum in Louisville, Kentucky, it felt right to dig back into the archives and come up with some fresh and unbelievable baseball facts.

Baseball is in Ripley Entertainment's DNA. Robert Ripley, our namesake was a huge baseball fan and before he created the venerable Believe it or Not! cartoon, he played sandlot and semi-pro baseball. After moving to New York City to pursue his artistic career as a sports illustrator, he tried out for the New York Giants and made the team in spring 1914. During his debut appearance in spring training, he broke his pitching arm, crushing his Major League baseball dreams. But it did not deter his love for the sport. Baseball was one of his favorite subjects to chronicle through the years.

You hold in your hands a book dedicated strictly to all things baseball. I have always appreciated that Ripley's Believe It or Not! only presents what is true and genuine. Ripley himself took great pride in presenting things so preposterous that their accuracy was immediately questioned. In keeping with the Ripley tradition, the amazing oddities and trivia presented in this book, to the best of our knowledge are all factual and genuine.

What you will soon be experiencing proves that, without a doubt, truth is definitely more bizarre and stranger than fiction. Sit back and read it, enjoy it, but most importantly, believe it!

Tim O'Brien
MARCH 2016

David Price signed a $217 million contract with the Red Sox in December 2015. The largest contract ever in MLB!

Laura, a four-ton elephant threw out the first pitch – a perfect strike - on August 12, 2005 in Comstock Park, Michigan for a West Michigan Whitecaps minor league game.

Sports Town USA! In 2015, MLB's Kansas City Royals and the NFL's Kansas City Chiefs made it to their respective playoffs in the same year for the first time ever! Believe it or Not!

The Royals used more pitchers (seven) in Game 1 of the 2015 World Series than they did in the entire 1985 World Series in which they used six.

> "Without a doubt, the most important person in the history of baseball is Jackie Robinson."
> – Filmmaker Ken Burns upon finishing the PBS film, *Jackie Robinson* in spring 2016.

Bartola Colon of the Mets became the oldest pitcher to lose a World Series game on October 27, 2015.

For the first time in baseball history, the 2015 World Series featured two expansion-era teams. The Mets joined the league in 1962 and the Royals joined in 1969.

The Texas Rangers used a record 40 different pitchers during the 2014 season and a record 64 position players during the year.

Ripley's — Believe It or Not!

SPARKS FLEW FROM THE MASK OF **ALEX AVILA**, A CATCHER FOR THE DETROIT TIGERS MAJOR LEAGUE BASEBALL TEAM, WHEN HE WAS HIT BY A BALL DURING A SEPT. 13, 2011 GAME!

No player for the Mets, founded in 1962, had hit three home runs in a home game until July 2015 when two of its players did. On the 12th, Kirk Nieuwenhuis hit three and on July 29, Lucas Duda did the same.

The Fable *of the Kid Who Shifted His Ideals to Golf and Finally Became a Baseball Fan and Took the Only Known Cure.* This black and white silent film from 1916 has the longest name of any baseball film ever!

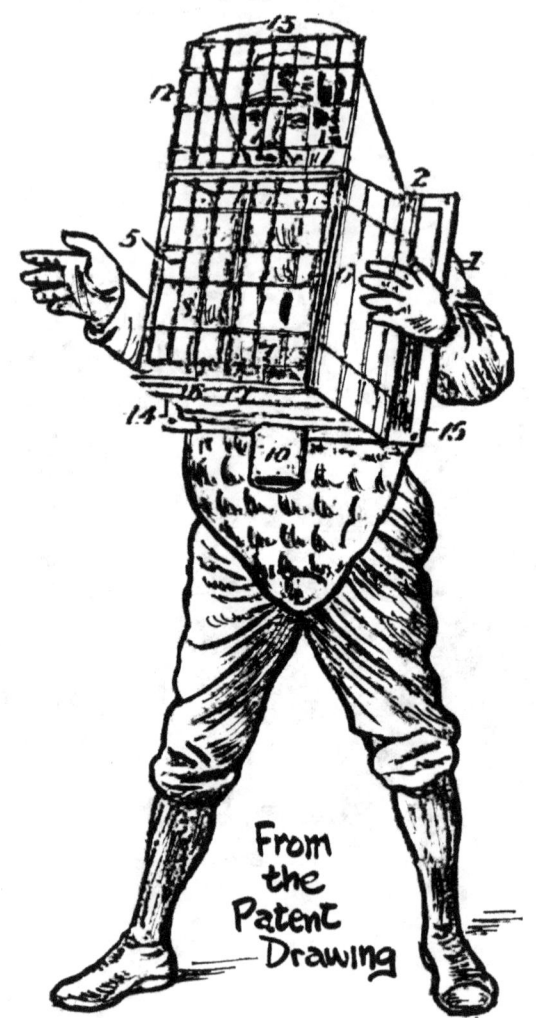

From the Patent Drawing

In 1904, **JAMES E. BENNETT** of Illinois, patented a **"BASE BALL CATCHER"**, designed so that baseball players could catch the ball *without* using their hands!

In all baseball history, the most runs scored in the Major Leagues was on June 29, 1897 when Chicago Colts (later the Cubs) beat the Louisville Colonels (folded in 1899) with 36 runs on 32 hits!

To celebrate his 100th home run on June 23, 1963, the Mets' Jimmy Piersall ran around the bases in the correct order but facing backward as he made the circuit.

Sports writer Zack Hample of New York City caught a baseball dropped from a helicopter flying 1,050 feet above him in July 2013. The ball plummeted toward him at speeds up to 95 mph on its 12-second journey into his mitt. Hample has also caught more than 6,800 foul and home run balls at 50 different ballparks across the country.

> "Probably the best thing that ever happened to me was going nuts."
> – Jimmy Piersall, on his chronic instability on the field.

Fruitful Outing! Brooklyn Dodgers' Wilbert Robinson was challenged to catch a ball dropped from an airplane flying over the Dodgers' spring training camp in 1914. Instead of a ball, the pilot substituted a small grapefruit and as Robinson caught the fruit it exploded in his glove knocking him down – covered with juice, seeds and rind.

Major League players were required to buy their own uniforms until 1912.

The Hagerstown (Maryland) Suns held one of the most bizarre minor league promotions ever. They gave away a free funeral – including embalming and a casket. Total value, $6,500.

Ruth's Café, a restaurant once operated by Babe Ruth's father, was located where Baltimore's Camden Yards now stands.

To celebrate the opening of spring training in 2013, Topps created a giant baseball card that stood nearly 90-feet tall and 60-feet wide and featured Detroit Tigers' Prince Fielder.

In 1882 outfielder Paul Hines of the Providence Grays became the first player to wear sunglasses while playing outfield.

WHAT DO THE **ATLANTA BRAVES** AND THE **WASHINGTON REDSKINS** HAVE IN COMMON? THEY WERE *BOTH* ONCE CALLED THE **BOSTON BRAVES** AND MADE FENWAY PARK, BOSTON, THEIR HOME STADIUM.

A 148-year old baseball card featuring a photo of the 1865 Brooklyn Atlantics amateur baseball club fetched $92,000 in a 2013 auction in Maine.

Nolan Ryan became the first to throw a pitch faster than 100 mph! It happened on August 20, 1974 in Anaheim Stadium.

LOUISVILLE SLUGGER
MUSEUM & FACTORY

Ripley's Believe it or Not! opened its first all-baseball exhibit inside the Louisville Slugger Museum & Factory in March 2016. Ripley's Believe it or Not! "Oddball" will run through the end of the year.

Louisville Slugger Museum & Factory opened on July 17, 1996. The bats have been made in Louisville for most of the company's history, except for the 22 years they were made in Indiana.

The first Louisville Slugger was made in 1884 after teenager Bud Hillerich made a replacement bat for his favorite team's star player.

Bud Hillerich's father J.F. Hillerich was originally against producing baseball bats in his shop because he disapproved of the gambling and alcohol that surrounded 19th century baseball.

Hillerich & Bradsby Co. was the first sporting goods company to secure athlete endorsements when Honus Wagner signed a contract in 1905.

More than 80% of all hitters in the Baseball Hall of Fame used Louisville Sluggers.

Wilson Sporting Goods paid $70 million in 2015 for Hillerich & Bradsby Co., which remains the sole maker of the Louisville Slugger wood bats.

The museum and factory has drawn more than four million guests since opening in 1996 and now averages more than 300,000 guests annually.

More than 6,000 unique bat models have been made over the years, customized for specific players, many of which are housed in the museum's "Bat Vault."

The Other BAT MATTER

Matt "Timber" Dopson snapped 19 baseball bats in half in 60 seconds on June 24, 2013 on a Guinness World Records Unleashed television show.

Dr. Mak Yuree Vajramuni from Bangladesh can shatter a bundle of three baseball bats with a single shin kick.

The Louisville Slugger bat that Babe Ruth used to hit the first home run in Yankee Stadium, sold at auction in December 2004 for $1.26 million.

Honus Wagner was the first player to have his signature on a bat – a Louisville Slugger.

Teams order nearly 150 bats each year for each of their hitters.

A ruling in 1888 allowing bats to have one flat side was revoked the following year.

Good Luck, Bad Luck. It's good luck to sleep with your bat if you're in a slump and its bad luck to lend your bat to a fellow player.

The heaviest bat used by a player on a consistent basis was 48 ounces by Hall of Fame outfielder Edd Roush. That's a full pound more than the standard bats used today.

Derek Jeter used the same exact bat model for every one of his 12,602 plate appearances over his 20-year career – the Louisville Slugger P72 model.

Being Possessive! The Phillies' Richie Ashburn took his bats home at night so they wouldn't be mixed with the team's other bats. He claimed to have slept with them in his bed. Later, he quipped that he had "slept with a lot of old bats."

Baseball's original 1845 rules mentions the word "bat" only one time with no descriptions or specifications. The first official guidelines for bats came in 1857.

Ty Cobb didn't tell management about a severe case of tonsillitis for fear of being taken out of the lineup. Instead, **HE HAD A HOTEL DOCTOR TAKE HIS TONSILS OUT,** without anesthetic or proper surgical equipment. He played seven innings the next day and got a hit.

Wigging out the opposition! 32,862 Los Angeles Angels fans wore red and white "rally wigs" for 10 minutes during the fifth inning of the game against the Astros in Anaheim. The June 2013 promotion set a new Guinness World Record.

Former Negro League players were selected as MVPs in the National League for seven consecutive years, 1953-1959.

New York Giants'

Bill Voiselle received special permission from the National League to wear #96 on his jersey as a way to honor his hometown of Ninety Six, South Carolina. At the time, it was the highest number ever worn in MLB.

> "Michael Jordan is leaving baseball to return to basketball. It is unclear whether the media will now refer to him by his old basketball nickname, 'Air Jordan,' or his more recent baseball nickname, 'Señor Crappy.'"
>
> – Comedian Norm MacDonald on *Saturday Night Live* in fall, 1994.

A sign hanging

in Detroit's Tiger Stadium over the visitor's clubhouse read: "Visitor's Clubhouse. No Visitors Allowed."

In the earliest days

of baseball, the game did not consist of nine innings. They played until one team scored a predetermined number of runs, usually 21.

What's a baseball, coach?

Herb Washington scored 33 runs and stole 31 bases in 105 games without batting, pitching, or fielding. With no prior baseball experience but an award winning track record, he was put on a two-year contract in 1974 with Oakland specifically to run the bases.

Minor league first baseman

David Denson came out as gay in late August 2015, making him the first openly gay active player affiliated with any Major League team.

DÉJÀ RUTH!

During the fourth game of both the 1926 and the 1928 World Series, **BABE RUTH** hit three home runs against the Cardinals.

Joe Engel, owner of the Chattanooga (Tennessee) Lookouts baseball team traded player Johnny Jones to Charlotte in return for a 25-pound turkey in 1931.

The big chomp! More than 39,000 fans ate potato chips simultaneously during the second inning of a game between the New York Mets and the Cincinnati Reds at Citi Field in New York in July 2009. The crunch could be heard throughout the ballpark.

> "I'll play out the string and leave baseball without a tear. A man can't play games his whole life."
> – Brooks Robinson

Following a bad inning in June 2007, pitcher Matt Elliott of the Mobile (Alabama) BayBears, went to the bathroom where he slammed the door hard in anger. The lock broke and he was trapped inside. The game was delayed as teammates tried to pry the door open but to avoid a forfeit, the team had to send in another pitcher. The door was broken down and Elliott escaped – more than 30 minutes after the game had ended.

Stealing them all! Six times in his career Ty Cobb reached first base on a single, then stole second, then stole third, and then stole home.

Believe It or Not! Willie Mays played in four World Series but never hit a home run.

Believe It or Not! 2015 $ALARIE$

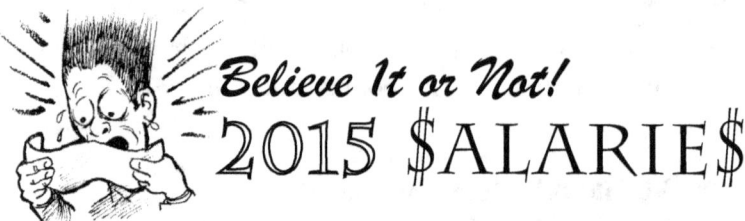

The Dodgers' opening day roster salary was $272,789,040, more than $57 million more than Marlins, Astros and Blue Jays – combined!

2015 World Series champs Royals had an opening day roster salary of $113,618,650, the 16th largest in MLB; the losing Mets came in with $101,409,244, the 21st largest.

The Dodgers' Clayton Kershaw and the Cubs' Jon Lester, both pitchers, were the two top salaried MLB players in 2015, with $30 million each, plus endorsements.

MLB had 28 players making salaries of more than $20 million; the NBA had eight; and the NFL only five. MLB minimum salary was $507,500.

Oakland Athletics' **PAT VENDITTE** is only the second ambidextrous player to pitch in the major leagues.

The first public address system was used by the New York Giants on August 25, 1929 when umpire Charles Rigler used a microphone mounted inside his mask to announce balls and strikes.

Seven up! Dock Ellis pitched for seven different managers on three different teams in 1977.

A robot created by the engineers at the University of Pennsylvania threw out the ceremonial first pitch at a 2011 game between the Phillies and the Brewers.

New Era Cap Company

created the world's largest hat mosaic in July 2011. Consisting of 1,875 official MLB caps, it promoted the brand's Fly Your Own Flag campaign encouraging consumers to make a statement with their New Era products.

"In 1997, when I was playing Double-A ball, I shared a car with my teammate, Armann Brown. It was a rental. It cost $6.99 a day. It was a Geo Prizm. We also shared an apartment. It was a rental. It cost $6.99 a day. It was a Geo Prizm."
– Torii Hunter, retired from the Twins

No glove, no problem. A spectator at a 2011 game between the Blue Jays and the Royals caught a foul ball – in his popcorn bucket.

Though he played more games with the A's, Reggie Jackson chose to wear a Yankees cap for his official Hall of Fame photo.

It took 134 years in MLB history for a player to hit homers from both sides of the plate on opening day. In the April 6, 2009 game, Diamondbacks' Felipe Lopez became the first. Just one inning later in the same game, Tony Clark become the second.

Believe It or Not! The odds were 1 in 32,678 that all 15 MLB home teams would win on the same day, but it happened for the first time on August 11, 2015.

The Minneapolis Metrodome is the only facility that has hosted a World Series, a Super Bowl, and a Final Four.

Reno Bertoia is the only player in the Major Leagues to be born on Elvis Presley's exact birth date – January 8, 1935.

Baseball is the fifth most dangerous sport, with 155,898 injuries a year. It follows basketball (512,213), cycling (485,669), football (418,260), and soccer (174,686).

Texas Rangers' Jose Canseco lost sight of a deep fly ball and as he dashed across the warning track, the ball bounced off his head and into the stands, giving the Indians' Carlos Martinez a home run. Texas lost by one run in that 1993 game.

> "He's got power enough to hit home-runs in any park, including Yellowstone."
> - Manager Sparky Anderson on Willie Stargell

The Cubs' Ken Holtzman pitched a no-hitter against the Braves on August 19, 1969 – without striking out a single batter!

Ripley's — Believe It or Not!

WHERE DO YOU WANT THIS FAT?

ON JULY 10, 1943, BROOKLYN DODGERS FANS ARRIVED AT EBBETS FIELD'S **KITCHEN FAT DAY** WITH 5,002 POUNDS OF FAT FOR THE WAR EFFORT.

No night games were permitted in 1943 due to war time blackout restrictions.

On an April 2, 1931, New York Yankees exhibition game, 17-year-old **Jackie Mitchell** struck out both Babe Ruth and Lou Gehrig in succession!

The New York Yankees have won the most World Series, 27, and lost the most World Series, 13.

Traveling fans. Josh Robbins of Redondo Beach, California traveled 14,212 miles in 2008 visiting all 30 MLB parks in just 26 days. The summer before, brothers Brigham and Todd Shearon from Windsor, Ontario, Canada, visited all 30 parks in 28 days, traveling 14,500 miles.

Ripley's — Believe It or Not!

Joe DiMaggio hit safely in 56 consecutive games in 1941 for the Yankees, a record that still stands through the 2015 season.

Paul Jones of Las Vegas started collecting baseball cards in 1997 and within 10 years had more than 520,500 in his collection.

John Jordon "Buck" O'Neil, a former coach and player, played in a minor league game in July 2006 – at the age of 94! He signed a one-game contract to play for the Kansas City T-Bones. He died three months later.

Eternal Image, a casket company in Michigan, produced coffins with logos and names of all 30 MLB teams from 2007 until they declared bankruptcy in 2012. They were also the official licensee of the Vatican, Star Trek, and the rock band KISS.

> "I didn't blow it. I used the power of suggestion. I yelled at it, go foul, go foul."
> – Mariners Lenny Randle after being accused of blowing a slow grounder into foul territory on May 27, 1981.

Satchel Paige is the oldest Major League player to have regularly played the game. He was 59 years and 80 days old when he last pitched for the Kansas City Athletics on September 25, 1965.

Paying Homage to
BILL "SPACEMAN" LEE

"The other day they asked me about mandatory drug testing. I said I believed in drug testing a long time ago. All through the '60s I tested everything."

Lee claimed that ingesting marijuana pancakes made him immune to the exhaust from buses during his regular jogs to Fenway Park.

"Because smoking isn't good for you. There are other ways, though. I like brownies."
- When asked in 2013 why he doesn't smoke weed anymore.

Ripley's — Believe It or Not!

The 65 year-old Lee became the oldest pitcher to win a professional baseball game when San Rafael Pacifics beat Maui Na Koa Ikaika on August 23, 2012. He had a one-day contract and pitched a nine inning complete game, also giving him the honor of being the oldest starting pitcher and the oldest pitcher to throw a complete game in professional baseball.

"I've just solidified myself as the best old guy on the planet."
– Lee after becoming the oldest player to win a game.

Jack Quinn of the Philadelphia Athletics is the oldest player ever in a World Series game. He was 47 years and 91 days old when he played on October 4, 1930.

Tony Suck retired in 1884 after two seasons of wretched play as a catcher, shortstop, and outfielder with the Baltimore Monumentals, Buffalo Bisons and the Chicago Browns. (Space here for your own joke!)

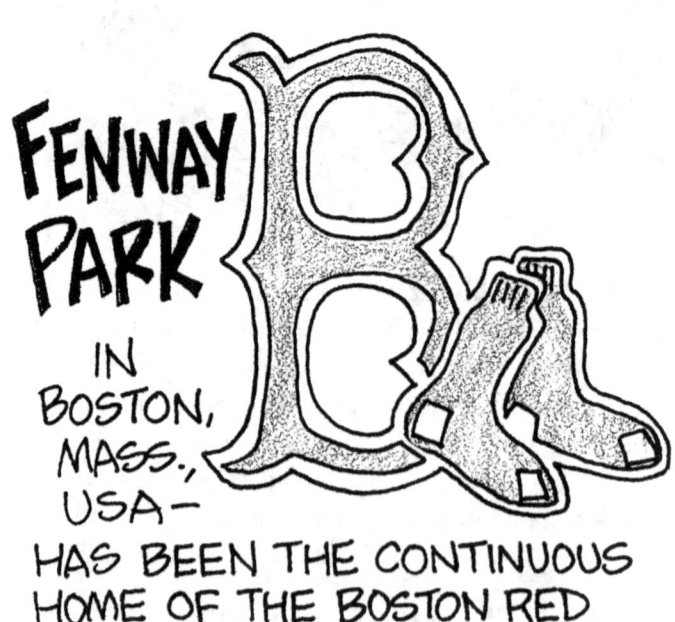

Fenway Park in Boston, Mass., USA — has been the continuous home of the Boston Red Sox of Major League Baseball since the stadium was built in 1912.

YUM.

American baseball fans consume about 26 million hot dogs a year — enough to circle a baseball diamond 36,000 times.

The New York Yankees became the first MLB franchise to hit 15,000 home runs when Brett Gardner hit one over the wall against the Blue Jays at Yankee Stadium on September 21, 2014.

What a year. Brandon Finnegan is the first to pitch in the College World Series and the MLB World Series the same year. The Texas Christian University pitcher was drafted by Kansas City Royals and later appeared in two games of the 2014 World Series.

While playing in the minor leagues in 1953, Don Zimmer was hit in the head with a ball and was unconscious for 13 days. He recovered, was called to the Major Leagues and three years later was hit and knocked unconscious again!

Ted Williams hit only one in-the-park home run during his career – against Cleveland in 1946, clinching the American League pennant for the Red Sox.

Louis Adamie, "Mr. Scoreboard," is in the Baseball Hall of Fame. He operated the Sportsman's Park and Busch Stadium scoreboards for the Cardinals and the Browns from 1941 to 1982. He also tracked every pitch in 4,350 games.

Believe It or Not! Stan Musial was making $100,000 a year with the Cardinals in the late 1950s, but was not happy about his quality of play during the 1960 season. He requested, and was granted, a salary cut of $20,000.

> "If your stomach disputes you, lie down and pacify it with cool thoughts."
> – A tip for staying young, Satchel Paige.

Pitcher perfect! During Catfish Hunter's 1968 perfect game against Minnesota, the Oakland acer was also nearly perfect with the bat. He hit three singles and drove in three runs.

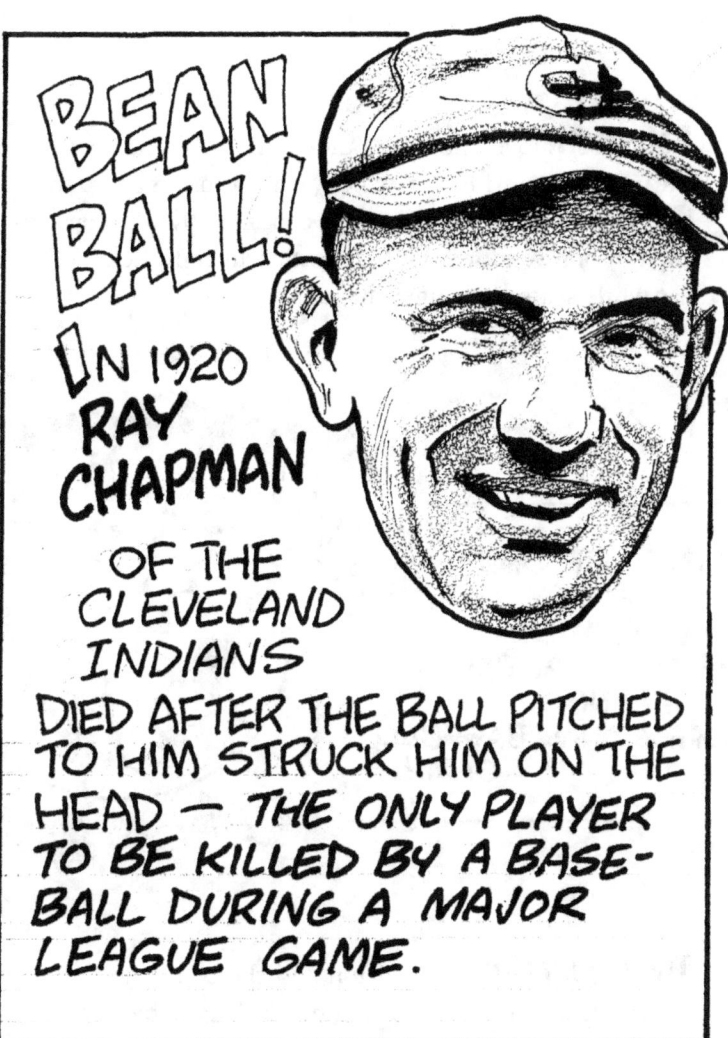

Canadian police arrested Dave Winfield after the game in which he threw a ball that killed a seagull during a Yankees and Blue Jays contest in 1983. Charges of Animal Cruelty were later dropped.

Babe Ruth loved hot dogs and would often eat them during a game. If he knew he wasn't going to be up to bat during an inning, he would occasionally walk over to the hot dog vendor from his position in right field and eat while seated amongst the fans.

There are only about 18 minutes of total action during a professional baseball game.

The popularity of television and the comfort of air conditioning nearly killed minor league baseball. In 1949, at its height, there were 59 minor leagues in 438 American cities, bringing in an attendance of 49 million spectators.

On the night in 2004 when the Boston Red Sox won their first world championship in 86 years – a lunar eclipse took place.

Ripley's—Believe It or Not!

The signed contract that sent Babe Ruth to New York from Boston in 1919 sold at a 2005 auction for $996,000.

> "Willie Mays' glove is where triples go to die."
> – Sportscaster Jim Murray.

A good day does not a season make! Stan Musial was the first MLB player to hit five homers in one day – but he never led his league in home runs.

The cap of Seattle pitcher Felix Hernandez fell off his head 11 times in one inning during his first outing in spring 2005. He contemplated various ways of keeping it on his head until he landed on the perfect solution – he cut his long and bushy hair!

During his incarceration in federal prison for tax evasion, Pete Rose earned 11 cents a day working in the prison's machine shop.

The total distance of the 73 home runs that Barry Bonds hit in 2001 was 23,809 feet, comparable to lining up 71,427 cheeseburgers in a row.

The Cleveland Indians were the first to wear numbers on their jerseys. They hit the field on June 26, 1916 with paper numbers pinned to their uniform. The numbers corresponded with the player's position on the field.

Believe It or Not! Barry Bonds hit more home runs after his 35th birthday than Roger Maris hit during his entire career.

MLB players munch on more than 300,000 bags of sunflower seeds each season.

Nancy Faust, the organist for the White Sox for 41 years, was the first ballpark organist to be honored with a Bobblehead Night, on September 18, 2010.

> "They usually show movies on a flight like that."
> – Announcer Ken Coleman's home run call.

A line-drive foul ball from the bat of Phillies' Richie Ashburn struck fan Alice Roth in the face breaking her nose on August 17, 1957. Play resumed and Ashburn fouled off the next pitch that hit her again as she was being carried out on a stretcher. Believe it or Not!

Dodger catcher John Roseboro was intentionally hit over the head with a bat by the Giants Juan Marichal, requiring 14 stitches. After he returned his batting average improved drastically for the rest of his career, causing one scribe to comment: "If more would have been written about (this incident), we may have had teammates all over the league whacking each other in the head with a bat!"

YOGI-isms

"Slump? I ain't in no slump. I just ain't hitting."

"If people don't want to come out to the ballpark, how are you going to stop them?"

"I'm not going to buy my kids an encyclopedia. Let them walk to school like I did."

More on page 38!

As a player, coach or manager, **YOGI BERRA** APPEARED IN 21 MAJOR LEAGUE BASEBALL WORLD SERIES AND HOLDS THE RECORDS FOR MOST SERIES PLAYED (14) AND MOST WINS (10).

Yogi Berra was more than an accidental philosopher. He was quite the ballplayer:
- Played 18 years with the Yankees, one with the Mets.
- With 10 rings, no one owns more MLB championship jewelry.
- Won three league MVP awards - 1951, '54 and '55.
- All-Star catcher 15 times.
- Elected to Hall of Fame 1972.
- 2,120 games, 7,555 regular season at-bats, 358 homers and only 414 strikeouts.
- 1,430 RBI's - no catcher has driven in more runs.

YOGI-isms

CONTINUED FROM PAGE 36

"You can observe a lot by watching."

"Nobody goes there anymore; it's too crowded."

"Always go to other people's funerals, otherwise they won't come to yours."

"So I'm ugly. I never saw anyone hit with his face."

Shoeless Joe Jackson could not read and could only write his own name. His wife signed nearly all the autograph requests he received by mail.

Big rain delay in 1945! For four days in a row, May 14-17 every single American League game was rained out.

Former Red Sox catcher and college football All-American Charlie Berry was an umpire in both the 1958 World Series and the 1958 NFL Championship game.

The Chicago Cubs in 1916 were the first team to allow fans to keep the foul balls hit into the stands.

George Brett won batting titles in 1976, 1980 and 1990 making him the only MLB player to win it in three different decades!

"There comes a time in every man's life, and I've had plenty of them."
— CASEY STENGEL

Indians fan Charlie Lupica spent 117 days sitting on top of a flagpole during the 1949 season waiting for the defending World Champion Indians to regain first place. He came down when they were mathematically eliminated on September 25.

> "Sure I played, did you think I was born age 70 sitting in a dugout trying to manage guys like you?"
> – Casey Stengel, to Mickey Mantle

Ichiro Suzuki was the first to hit an inside-the-park home run in an All-Star Game - in 2007.

In its 46 years of existence, the San Diego Padres remains the only existing franchise in Major League Baseball that has not had a pitcher toss a no-hitter.

Dodgers' Don Drysdale played himself in an episode of *The Brady Bunch* in 1970. In "The Dropout," he convinces Greg not to drop out of school to pursue a career in baseball.

Pete Rose hit more pitches thrown by Phil Niekro than any other pitcher in the Major Leagues - 64.

Brad Turney of Alexandria, Louisiana, played all nine positions for the minor league Alexandria Aces, during a single regulation game on June 29, 2007.

Ripley's — Believe It or Not!

AT ANGELS STADIUM ON SEPTEMBER 14, 1990, **KEN GRIFFEY** AND HIS SON, **KEN GRIFFEY JR.**, HIT BACK-TO-BACK HOME RUNS!

Ken Griffey Jr. received 99.3% of all votes, the highest voting percentage ever in the history of the Baseball Hall of Fame voting. As part of the Class of 2016, he received 437 of the 440 votes cast.

Believe It or Not! Ken Griffey Jr. amassed the highest number of votes ever— 50,045,065 — in voting for the 2015 All-Star Game!

Born without a right hand, Jim Abbott had a 10-year MLB pitching career including two years with the Yankees where he tossed a no-hitter against Cleveland on September 4, 1993.

THE NEW YORK METS HAVE PLAYED THREE OF THE LONGEST GAMES IN MLB® HISTORY, ONE JULY 1985 GAME VS. THE ATLANTA BRAVES LASTED 8 HOURS AND 15 MINUTES, ENDING AT 3:55 A.M. WITH A NY WIN!

Maury Wills of the Dodgers was the first player to bat on Astroturf. It was opening day on April 18, 1966 in the Houston Astrodome.

> "If horses can't eat it, I don't want to play on it."
> – Phillies' Dick Allen expressing his disdain for artificial turf.

A recording of "Take Me Out to the Ball Game" was embedded in the cardboard cover of Wheaties in 1954 that could be cut out and played on any record player.

Baseballs are stored in a humidor at the mile high and very dry Coors Field to keep them at the same level of moisture as those found in other MLB stadiums.

In Denver's Coors Field, home of the Rockies, row 20 in the upper 300s sections is located at exactly one mile above sea level. All seats in that row are purple.

Madison Bumgarner of the SF Giants is the first player in MLB to pitch more than 50 innings during a World Series. He threw 52.2 innings and was the 2014 World Series MVP.

Roberto Clemente retired in 1972 and died on the last day of that year in a plane crash in Puerto Rico while delivering humanitarian aid to earthquake victims in Nicaragua. He was buried at sea.

Chief Noc-A-Homa, the former screaming Indian mascot of the Milwaukee and Atlanta Braves "lived" in a teepee in the bleacher section and once set it on fire while trying to send smoke signals. Nearby fans doused the flames with beer.

> "The ball was small sometimes. The ball was large sometimes. Sometimes I saw the catcher. Sometimes I didn't."
> – Pirates' Dock Ellis describing what it was like pitching a no-hitter on June 12, 1970 while tripping on LSD.

Following 15 years as a player and two years as a coach, Moe Berg, who was often referred to as the "brainiest guy in baseball," became a spy for the U.S. in 1943.

Double dipping. Cal Hubbard is in the Pro Football Hall of Fame (1963) as a player and the Baseball Hall of Fame (1976) as an umpire. Believe It or Not!

Jackie Robinson's number 42 was retired across all of MLB on April 15, 1997. Players whose number was 42 on that day were allowed to continue wearing it until they retired. The Yankees' Mariano Rivera, who retired in 2013, was the last player permitted to regularly wear #42.

The U.S. has won only one Olympic gold medal in baseball – in 2000.

Presidential Quotes

"One of the great things about living here (in the White House) is that you don't have to sign up for a baseball fantasy camp to meet your heroes. It turns out they come here." – George W. Bush

"I never dreamed about being President; I wanted to be Willie Mays." – George W. Bush

"Our national pastime - that is if you discount political campaigning." – Ronald Reagan

"I don't know a lot about politics, but I do know a lot about baseball." – Richard Nixon

"I had a life-long ambition to be a professional baseball player, but nobody would sign me up." – Gerald Ford

"What do you imagine the American people would think of me if I wasted my time going to the ball game?" – Grover Cleveland

Ripley's — Believe It or Not!

After a baseball stuck in his glove during a game on June 6, 1999, New York Yankee's player **Orlando "El Duque" Hernandez** threw an out by tossing the glove and the ball together.

Harry Truman attended more MLB games than any other sitting president – 16!

U.S. President Bill Clinton and VP Al Gore attended Cal Ripken's 2,131st game on September 6, 1995, becoming the first President and VP to attend a game together while in office.

President Warren Harding played ball with future MLB players when he was younger, owned a minor league baseball team as an adult, and was on hand to see the first Yankee Stadium shutout.

President John F. Kennedy sat through every inning of every game he was able to attend during his presidency.

Ken Griffey Jr. hit 351 home runs during President Bill Clinton's eight years in the White House. Babe Ruth hit 248 during President Calvin Coolidge's White House tenure.

NUMBER OF U.S. PRESIDENTS WHO HELD OFFICE BETWEEN THE YEARS BOSTON WON THE WORLD SERIES, 1918 AND 2004.

A BASEBALL STRUCK BY A BAT ACCELERATES AT 3,000 TIMES THE FORCE OF GRAVITY, 30 TIMES FASTER THAN A **BALLISTIC MISSILE!**

Unlike other sports, baseball has no time limit or clock.

During World War II, the U.S. military designed a grenade to be the size and weight of a baseball, so that any young American man could "properly" throw it.

BILL VIRDON
WON 142 GAMES
AS THE MANAGER
OF THE 1974 & 1975
NEW YORK YANKEES,
BUT
NEVER WON A GAME
AT YANKEE STADIUM!

The Albuquerque Isotopes, the Triple-A affiliate of the Dodgers named themselves after the fictitious minor league team on TV's *The Simpsons* when they moved from Calgary, Canada in 2003.

Joe DiMaggio played in the World Series 10 of his 13 MLB seasons and Yogi Berra in 14 of his 19 years.

The lights from a circus tent set up in the parking lot of Raymond James Stadium caused cancellation of a Florida State League game between the Tampa Yankees and the Clearwater Threshers on August 7, 2015.

Below the belt! Johnny Bench had his protective cup shattered by a pitched ball seven times!

"It could be, it might be...it is! A home run!"
– Announcer Harry Caray's home run call.

Dodgers' outfielder and prankster Jay Johnstone once replaced all the signed photos of celebrities in Tommy Lasorda's office with signed pictures of himself.

During his 22-year career, Mel Ott hit 323 home runs in the Polo Grounds as a New York Giant, the most homers any player has ever hit in one ballpark.

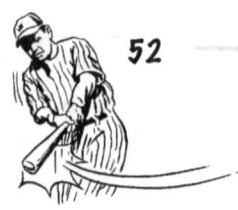

BASEBALL PITCHER **RAY CALDWELL** OF THE CLEVELAND INDIANS WAS HIT BY LIGHTNING DURING A GAME IN 1919 — AND CONTINUED TO PLAY!

Jockey brand underwear model Jim Palmer was known as "Cakes" early in his career, thanks to his penchant for eating big stacks of hotcakes every day he was scheduled to pitch.

Mr. Coffee's first spokesman was Joe DiMaggio.

As a Dodger, Pee Wee Reese played in 44 World Series games – every one against the Yankees!

> "You couldn't pitch a tent."
> – heckle directed to a pitcher

Honus Wagner was the first player to reach 3,000 hits in the 20th century – on June 9, 1914.

The first pinch hitter in baseball history was Mickey Welch, a pitcher for the New York Giants, on August 10, 1889. He batted for teammate Hank O'Day in the bottom of the fifth inning and struck out.

Cincinnati's Hall of Fame catcher Johnny Bench hammered 45 home runs in 1970 - 15 at Crosley Field, 15 at Riverfront Stadium and 15 on the road.

Only one of Hank Aaron's 755 home runs was an inside-the-park homer.

DOUBLE DUTY PLAYERS

Among those selected in the 1971 Major League amateur draft were future NFL quarterbacks Archie Manning, Joe Theisman, and Steve Bartkowski.

Among those selected in the 1979 Major League amateur draft were future NFL quarterbacks Dan Marino, John Elway, Curt Warner, and Jay Schroeder.

Gene Conley played on the Milwaukee Braves World Series Championship team of 1957 and during 1959-61 on the Boston Celtics NBA Champion teams.

As a punter for the 1994 Nebraska Cornhuskers National Championship football team, Darin Erstad finished 14th in the nation with a 42.6 yard average. Following college, he spent 14 years in the big leagues and was selected to the American League All-Star team twice, 1998 and 2000. Following his retirement he returned to Nebraska where he is currently the Cornhusker's head baseball coach.

Ripley's —— Believe It or Not!®

DEION SANDERS
IS THE ONLY ATHLETE TO PLAY **IN BOTH** THE **SUPER BOWL**, FOR THE SAN FRANCISCO 49ERS (1995) AND THE DALLAS COWBOYS (1996), AND THE **WORLD SERIES**, FOR THE ATLANTA BRAVES (1992).

A great week! Deion Sanders hit a home run for the Yankees on September 5, 1989, then had a 68-yard touchdown run for the Atlanta Falcons on September 9.

Baseball Hall of Fame pitchers Ferguson Jenkins and Bob Gibson both played basketball with the Harlem Globetrotters.

At 44 years and three months, Nolan Ryan is the oldest to pitch a no-hitter, beating Toronto on May 1, 1991, 3-0. Only three others over 40 years old have thrown no-hitters: Warren Spahn, Cy Young and Randy Johnson.

> "Why do we sing 'Take Me Out to the Ballgame' when we're already there?"
> – George Carlin

In search of perfection! Of the 292 no-hitters in MLB through the 2015 season, only 23 have been perfect games.

First time in 50 years! On May 19, 2013, Diamondback Gerardo Parra homered on the game's first pitch and no further runs were scored in the game. Cincinnati's Pete Rose did the same thing with the first pitch in a 1-0 win against New York in 1963.

The youngest starting lineup in MLB history took the field on September 27, 1963. The Houston Colt .45s fielded an all-rookie lineup with 19 being the average age of its players.

Brotherly love. The largest group of siblings to all play in the Major Leagues was the Delahanty family – Ed, Jim, Joe, Tom and Frank, all playing between the years 1888 and 1915.

Umpires kept a close eye on Don Sutton, as he was known for scuffing pitches. Once while inspecting his glove for sandpaper, the ump found a small note that read. "You're getting warm, but it's not here."

Believe It or Not! Pitcher Rollie Fingers was elected into the Hall of Fame with a lifetime losing record of 114-118.

Believe it! Pitcher Rube Marquard of the New York Giants kicked off the 1912 season with 19 consecutive wins, a record that still stands through 2015.

THE NUMBER OF HOT DOGS BABE RUTH ONCE ATE BETWEEN GAMES OF A DOUBLEHEADER.

CINCINNATI REDS PITCHER **JOHNNY VANDER MEER** IS THE ONLY MLB PITCHER TO THROW CONSECUTIVE NO-HITTERS, ACCOMPLISHED IN 1938.

Nice way to close out a career! Dave Kingman is the only Major Leaguer to hit more than 30 home runs in his last season, hitting 35 for Oakland in 1986.

The Boston Red Sox have never been swept in a World Series. They have played in 12 and lost four, with all four losing outings going seven games.

Sean Casey contributed the first hit at two new ballparks – Miller Park in Milwaukee and PNC Park in Pittsburgh.

Bart Giamatti, the commissioner who banned Pete Rose from baseball is the father of actor Paul Giamatti.

A major life insurance company published a study that showed Major League baseball players, compared with males from the general population, have significantly longer life spans. The study also revealed that third basemen live longer than other ballplayers, while shortstops have the shortest life span.

> "Catching a fly ball is a pleasure, but knowing what to do with it after you catch it is a business."
> – Tommy Henrich

The illusion of Hollywood! The logos on the hat and uniform Gary Cooper wore as he portrayed Lou Gehrig in *Pride of the Yankees* were reversed for filming and then the negatives flipped for the final version of the film. It was easier that way for the right-handed Cooper to play the left-handed Gehrig.

Mr. Met, the New York Mets' mascot was the first MLB mascot to depict a real human, rather than an animal or creature.

HOMER BAILEY AND RYAN DEMPSTER BECAME THE FIRST MAJOR LEAGUE BASEBALL PITCHERS TO FACE EACH OTHER ON THEIR **BIRTHDAYS** WHEN CINCINNATI PLAYED CHICAGO ON MAY 3, 2012.

Ripley's —— Believe It or Not!

Bob Feller pitched a no-hitter on opening day, April 16, 1940 - the only MLB pitcher to ever do so.

Joe Pignatano, a player with the Fort Worth team in the Texas League during the 1950s hit a home run only to be told that he hit out of turn, the run did not count and he was out. Officially he was next up, so he stepped back into the box and hit the next pitch over the wall. This one counted.

Unloading the bat. On September 7, 1974, Yankee Graig Nettles swung at a pitch, the top of the bat flew off and six Superballs flew out. He was called out and ejected from the game.

SCARY COLLISION. OW!

In a July 5, 1924 game against the Washington Senators at Griffith Stadium, Babe Ruth collided with a cement wall and was knocked out for five minutes. He got up, stayed in the game and had two more hits.

BASEBALL IN 2015 — A long HOT season!

A Major League hitter today strikes out 48.8% more often than a batter did 30 years ago.

Strikeouts per game have risen during the past 10 years, the last eight of which set new records.

At 2:53, the average MLB, nine-inning game was the shortest since 2011.

Ground ball rates were at their highest ever, at 46.3%

League average fastball velocity rose to 92 mph.

Mud Hens' Mike Hessman hit homer #433 in August, a new minor league record.

Ripley's Believe It or Not!

During a record 27-year career, **NOLAN RYAN** struck out 5,714 batters— nearly 1,000 more than strikeout runner-ups Randy Johnson (4,875) and Roger Clemens (4,672)!

Ripley's — Believe It or Not!

Ichiro Suzuki is the only player to average more than 200 hits over his first 14 seasons. From 2001 through 2014, he posted 2,844 hits.

What a relief! Hoyt Wilhelm was the first relief pitcher elected to the Hall of Fame.

Old Yankee Stadium hosted exactly 100 World Series games.

Boston was the first MLB team to win five World Series, winning their fifth in 1918.

Detroit's Hank Greenberg was the first player to win MVP awards at two different positions: First base in 1935; Outfielder in 1940.

Casey Stengel is the only man to wear the uniform of all four of New York's Major League teams: Dodgers, Giants, Yankees, and the Mets.

> "You get less hits than an Amish web site."
> – heckle directed to a hitter

Todd Zeile was the first player to hit home runs for 11 different teams.

The Ball Game, a short documentary produced in 1898 is the first known film about baseball.

Built in 1910,
Rickwood Field, located in Birmingham, Alabama, is the oldest surviving professional baseball park in the U.S. and is listed on the National Register of Historic Places.

"Baseball is a game where a curve is an optical illusion, a screwball can be a pitch or a person, stealing is legal, and you can spit anywhere you like except in the umpire's eyes or on the ball."
– Jim Murray

The Brooklyn Dodgers
was the first team to buy their own airplane – in 1957!

March 31, 1996
- First time opening day occurred before April 1.

Oakland's Johnny Damon
hit one of the most bizarre ground rules double ever. The ball landed fair but rolled into foul territory – right into an empty beer cup that had been thrown from the stands.

Phillies pitcher
Harry Coveleski carried bologna in his back pocket and chewed on it throughout the game.

Ripley's — Believe It or Not!

On August 1, 1957, in Omaha, NE, minor league player **GLEN GORBOUS** threw a baseball 445 ft. 10 in. — a record that still stands today!

Quirks, *Rituals* & Superstitions

When he was struggling to get a hit, Yankee Jason Giambi would put on a female's gold thong.

Mets' pitcher R.A. Dickey names each one of his bats with creative and wacky names, such as Orchrist the Goblin Cleaver.

Roger Clemens made it a point to touch the Babe Ruth plaque at Monument Park prior to every home game he pitched for the Yankees.

Stan Musial would eat the same breakfast on every game day - an egg followed by two pancakes, and then another egg.

Pitcher Justin Verlander visits Taco Bell before every game and eats the same meal - three crunchy taco supremes, no tomato, a cheesy gordita crunch and a Mexican pizza, no tomato.

Before each game he is scheduled to start, pitcher Matt Garza has a meal at Popeye's chicken.

Nyjer Morgan wore blue argyle socks under his regulation socks during every game.

Joe DiMaggio would make sure that he touched second base on his way from the dugout to center field.

Ripley's — Believe It or Not!

Mark McGwire wore the same protective cup that he did in high school throughout his 16 year career in the majors.

Every time Lenny Dykstra would hit into an out, he would exchange his batting gloves for a new pair.

Turk Wendell never went to the mound to pitch without having exactly four pieces of black licorice in his mouth.

Pitcher Don Robinson insisted on picking the ball up off the ground before he began to pitch the inning. If someone would toss it to him, he would let it fall to the ground, then pick it up.

When he pitched for the Chicago Cubs, Ryan Dempster went to the same Italian restaurant the night before every start that he made at Wrigley Field.

The night before he is set to start, pitcher Derek Holland goes to Wendy's and orders $30 worth of food.

Wade Boggs would take batting practice at exactly 5:17 before a night game.

SUPERSTITIOUS FORMER **RED SOX** THIRD BASEMAN **WADE BOGGS** ALWAYS FIELDED EXACTLY 150 GROUNDERS DURING WARM UPS AND ATE CHICKEN ON GAME DAYS.

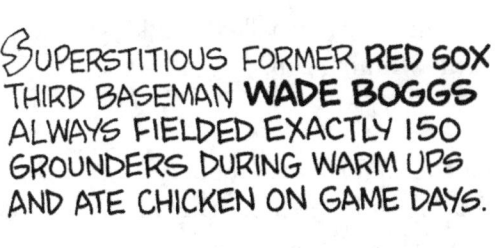

In 1970 **ALAN FISH** WAS KILLED WHEN **MANNY MOTA** HIT A BASEBALL INTO THE CROWD AT DODGER STADIUM IN LA — THE ONLY PERSON EVER TO HAVE BEEN KILLED BY A BALL HIT INTO THE STANDS, EVEN THOUGH AN AVERAGE OF 30 SUCH BALLS ARE HIT IN EACH MAJOR LEAGUE GAME.

Nationals' pitcher Mike Stanton was credited with a loss without throwing a single pitch on July 15, 2005! He went to the mound with bases loaded in the bottom of the ninth, score tied. He immediately balked, walking the batter and sending in the winning run.

Ron LeFlore was serving a term for armed robbery when he was signed by the Tigers in 1973. During his subsequent nine years in the Major Leagues, he stole 455 bases and was caught stealing only 142 times.

Ron Hunt of the Expos was hit 243 times by pitches during his career – 50 of them in 1971!

The Cincinnati Red Stockings became the first all-professional team in 1869 and went undefeated, 65-0 that year turning in the only perfect season in professional baseball history.

Every U.S. state and more than 45 countries, have had at least one player make it to the Major Leagues. Alaska has had the fewest with 11; California the most with 2,145.

There were six no-hit games in 1990, a record for the most ever in a single MLB season.

"I only have one superstition. I touch all the bases when I hit a home run."

– BABE RUTH

Men of Endurance

No Days Off! In 1962, Maury Wills played in 165 games for the Los Angeles Dodgers.

During his 55-year career as a baseball announcer, Ernie Harwell announced more than 8,300 Major League games for the Brooklyn Dodgers, New York Giants, Baltimore Orioles and the Detroit Tigers.

Playing for the Reds, Phillies and Expos between 1963 and 1986, Pete Rose was at bat 14,053 times and played in 3,562 games.

Joe DiMaggio played every inning of every All-Star Game from 1936 to 1942.

Long Squat! Yankee Yogi Berra caught all 22 innings in a game against Detroit on June 24, 1962, at age 37!

Derek Jeter played in a record 158 postseason games with the New York Yankees between 1995 and 2014.

The longest game, by innings, in Major League history was a 25-inning affair on May 8, 1984 when the Chicago White Sox beat the Milwaukee Brewers, 7-6.

Ripley's—Believe It or Not!

George Bradley pitched all 64 games for the St. Louis Browns in 1876 during the first season of the National League. He won 45 of them, pitched 16 shutouts and threw the first recognized no-hitter.

52-year-old Mike Filippone of Babylon, New York, batted for 24 consecutive hours in June 2013 during which time he hit nearly 10,000 balls. Earlier, in August 2009, he swung at 7,000 pitches over a period of 13 ½ hours.

Fifty players took part in an amateur baseball game that lasted 60 hours, 11 minutes and 32 seconds in July 2012 in O'Fallon, Missouri, making it the longest game ever. During the marathon, 169 innings were played and 451 runs scored.

Cal Ripken Jr. of the Orioles played 2,632 consecutive games between May 30, 1982 and September 19, 1998.

WHEW!!! JUST ONE! IN 1916, THE CHICAGO CUBS AND THE CINCINNATI REDS PLAYED A NINE-INNING GAME WITH JUST ONE BASEBALL!

Believe It or Not! The Chicago Cubs have more wins than any professional team in any sport – 10,608.

The Reds' Adam Dunn smacked a homer out of Cincinnati's Great American Ballpark on August 10, 2004 and it landed in the Ohio River – on the Kentucky side, making Dunn the only person to hit a home run into another state.

Great start! Pitcher Mike Parrot won on opening day, 1980 for the Mariners, but then proceeded to lose every game he pitched for the rest of the season, for a 1-16 record.

Umpire Tom Gorman was buried in 1986 in his uniform with an indicator set in his hand at a 3-2 count.

The life of a baseball in a MLB game today is about four pitches.

> "When a pitcher is throwing a spitball, don't worry and don't complain. Just hit the dry side like I do."
> – Stan Musial

Triple play! Playing in an amateur game in Portsmouth, Ohio in May 2008, triplets Howard, John and Matt Harcha all hit home runs – in the order of their birth from oldest to youngest.

ROY HALLADAY IS THE ONLY PITCHER IN MLB HISTORY TO TOSS A NO-HITTER IN BOTH THE REGULAR AND POST SEASONS!

The Florida Marlins is the only team that travels north to spring training.

The first All-Star Game was played at Chicago's Comiskey Park as an adjunct event to the Century of Progress, the 1933 World's Fair. A capacity crowd of 47,595 showed up.

> "I swing big, with everything I've got. I hit big or I miss big. I like to live as big as I can."
> – Babe Ruth

In the years between their World Championship seasons of 1985 and 2015, Kansas City lost more games than any team in MLB.

St. Louis Cardinals' Matt Holliday was forced out of a game on August 22, 2011 when a moth became lodged in his ear. Trainers had to extract the creature with tweezers.

Babe brings big bucks! At a 2012 auction, Babe Ruth's circa-1920 Yankees jersey sold for $4.42 million; his 1934 cap went for $537,278; and one of the bats he used in the 1920s brought in $591,007.

Arizona Diamondbacks' Mark Reynolds hit home runs on August 3, his birthday, in both 2009 and 2010.

Ripley's — Believe It or Not!

Cincinnati Reds' PETE ROSE hit 160 career home runs and only one was a grand slam!

Battering Bambino, Herman the Great, High Priest of Swat, King of Clout, King of Swing, Sultan of Swat, Wizard of Whack – all euphemisms for Babe Ruth.

Nolan Ryan became baseball's first million dollar a year man in 1979.

A measuring error in 1893 – why the pitching mound is now exactly 60 feet, 6 inches from home plate.

Prior to 1872, pitchers were required to throw underhand. Their purpose wasn't to get outs but to serve up pitches to be put in play.

Baseball Hall-of-Famer **TED WILLIAMS** (1918-2002) of the Boston Red Sox, and his son **JOHN-HENRY** (1968-2004), are both cryogenically frozen at a facility in Arizona.

Deep in debt, Lenny Dykstra sold his 1986 World Series ring for $56,762 in 2009 to pay creditors.

Prefers to be a pierogi. Andrew Kurtz's job was to dress up like a pierogi and race around the stadium for the Pittsburgh Pirates, but in 2010, he was fired for posting negative comments about the team on Facebook. He quickly found another job running around as a hot dog for a nearby minor league baseball team. However, before he donned the frankfurter suit, the Pirates rehired him saying his firing was a mistake.

Yankee Stadium was the first baseball field to be called a stadium. Prior to its 1923 opening, most of the game sites were called fields, grounds or parks.

> "Aw, c'mon, how could he lose the ball in the sun? He's from Mexico."
> – Harry Caray

Pro football Hall of Famer Greasy Neal was quite the sportsman. During his life he won two NFL titles as head coach of the Philadelphia Eagles, coached Washington & Jefferson University in the 1922 Rose Bowl, and played eight years in the majors including the 1919 World Series.

It took nine non-strike pitches for an umpire to issue a base-on-balls – in 1879!

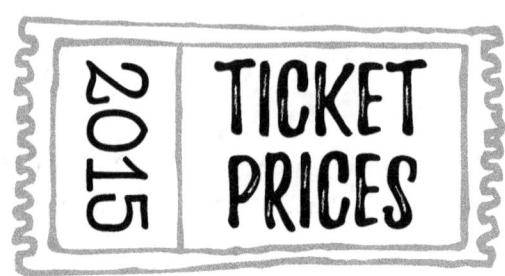

MLB average, non-premium ticket price was $28.94.

Boston retained its position as having the most expensive ticket, with an average of $52.34.

Arizona had the cheapest average seat cost of $17.98.

World Series teams. Royals had an average ticket cost of $29.76; the Mets, $25.30.

A TICKET TO THE FIRST ALL-STAR GAME IN **1933** COST **$1.10**

The wife of Yankees' Don Larsen filed for divorce on October 8, 1956, the same day he pitched the only perfect game in World Series history.

Following the game, Don Larsen had his hat, glove and ball from his World Series perfect game cast in silver and in 2002, he sold them at auction for $120,750 to help his grandchildren pay for college.

Bagger, dink, one-bagger, squib, banjo hit and plunker - a few of the nearly 40 names used to describe a hit single.

WHAT COULD POSSIBLY GO WRONG?

Thanks to a (no-limit) 10-cent beer night promotion on June 4, 1974, Cleveland had to forfeit a game. Rowdy fans rushed the field and attacked several Texas Rangers players, along with umpire Nestor Chylak.

MINOR LEAGUE BASEBALL TEAM THE **BOWIE BAYSOX** HOSTED **BACK HAIR APPRECIATION NIGHT** ON JULY 30, 2015— FREE BACK WAXES WERE PROVIDED.

Victories don't come easy. That's what Toronto Blue Jays' pitcher Joseph "Jo-Jo" Reyes discovered between June 13, 2008 and May 30, 2011. He started 28 games without a single win!

No cracks here! MLB umpires are required to wear black underwear, in case they split their pants.

84

Pitcher **Derek Moore** of Wheelersburg, OH, held a perfect high school career record — 36 wins, 0 losses and 2 back-to-back state championships!

The most incredible find of baseball cards ever took place in Defiance, Ohio in 2012 when Karl Kissner uncovered a soot-covered box of 700 cards from 1910 in his late grandfather's attic. The cards, all in excellent condition, are estimated to bring up to $3 million at auctions planned to take place over the next several years.

In 2014/2015, there was a 40% turnover rate for general managers in MLB.

Spoiler alert! Cesar Tovar ruined no-hitters for five different pitchers during his 12-year MLB career by getting the only hit in a one-hit game.

"The funny thing about these uniforms is that you hang them in the closet and they get smaller and smaller."
– Curt Flood

Hisashi Iwakuma became the second Japanese-born pitcher in the MLB to throw a no-hitter on August 11, 2015.

Fewer than half of the nearly 17,000 players who have played in the Major Leagues ever hit a home run.

Pinstripes didn't appear on Yankee uniforms until April 22, 1915.

The most runs scored by one team after 1900 is 30! On August 22, 2007, the Rangers walloped the Orioles 30-3 scoring all their runs in just four innings.

Several MLB teams appear to be losing fans at a rapid pace. Steep decreases in home attendance from 2006-2015 shows that the Phillies were down 29.5%; Indians, 28.4%; White Sox, 24.1%; and the Astros, 23.2%.

Good date! Three future hall of famers were born on January 31: Nolan Ryan, Ernie Banks, Jackie Robinson.

BELIEVE IT OR NOT!

Troy Tulowitzki of the Colorado Rockies HIT ONE PITCH **TWICE** WITH ONE SWING OF HIS BAT for a single to left field during a game with the Yankees on June 25, 2011.

Ripley's —— Believe It or Not!

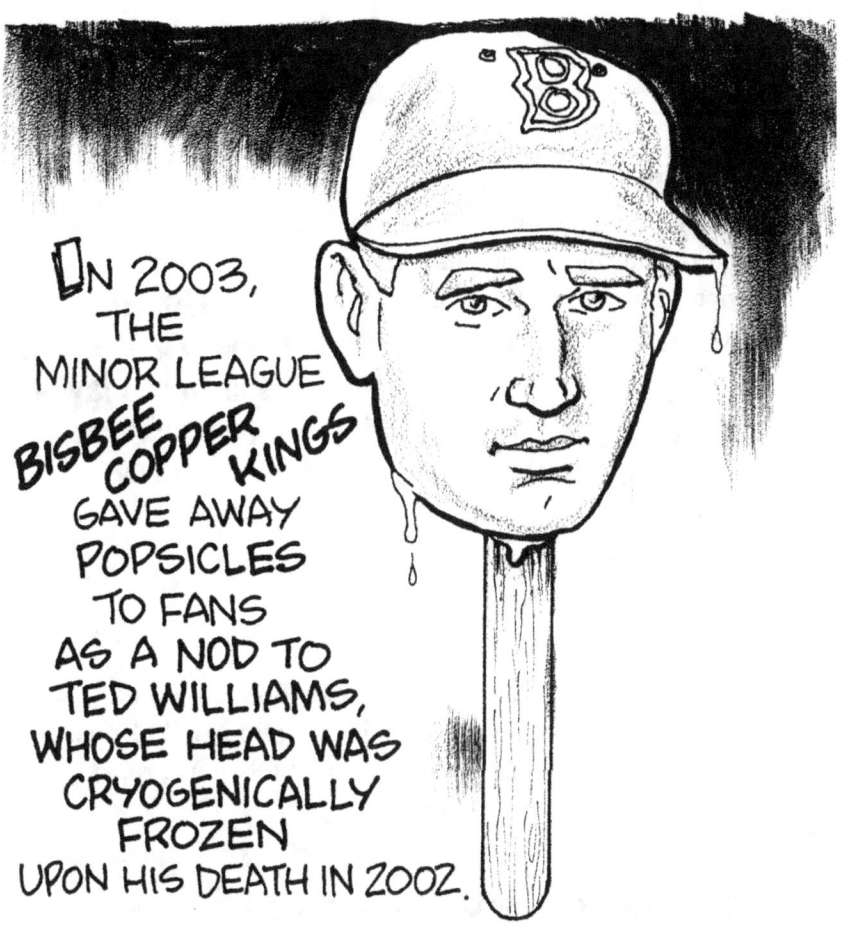

In 2003, the minor league BISBEE COPPER KINGS gave away popsicles to fans as a nod to Ted Williams, whose head was cryogenically frozen upon his death in 2002.

A swarm of bees invaded Angels Stadium on September 22, 2013, causing two game delays between Los Angeles and the Seattle Mariners. Most of the fans fled the stands or pulled blankets over their heads while a beekeeper lured the stingers away – with a bucket of honey!

Ouch! Umpires did not wear chest protectors until 1885.

Sign up this fan! Caleb Lloyd caught two home run balls in the same inning during a Cincinnati Reds victory over the Atlanta Braves in May 2012.

Oops, sorry honey! The Orioles' Jay Gibbons hit a line drive foul ball into the stands on September 23, 2006 hitting his wife, Laura.

> "With the money I'm making, I should be playing two positions."
> – Pete Rose

By the numbers! Barry and Bobby Bonds are the most successful father-son combination in MLB history. Combined, they lead all others with 1,094 home runs; 3,020 RBI's; and 975 stolen bases.

Curt Schilling's father died before Curt made the big leagues. To honor him, Curt reserved a seat for his father at every home game he started.

Swing baby! The Milwaukee Brewers became the first team in MLB history in 2001 to record more strikeouts - 1,399, than hits - 1,378.

Bank robber John Dillinger played professional baseball as a second baseman in small town leagues and while in prison, played for the prison team.

Ripley's — Believe It or Not!

What happened? Dal Maxville had 116 hits for the Cardinals during the 1968 season but went 0-22 in that year's World Series.

Time to buy a lottery ticket! The Cardinals' Reggie Sanders hit his 11th home run of the season, stole his 11th base and hit his 11th double all in the same game – on June 11, 2004.

NEW YORK GIANTS OUTFIELDER **BOBBY THOMSON** HIT THE GAME-WINNING HOME RUN KNOWN AS THE "SHOT HEARD 'ROUND THE WORLD" IN 1951— THE BASEBALL HAS YET TO BE FOUND!

Future Hall of Famer Dave Winfield was born on October 3, 1951, the same day of Thomson's big hit in the Polo Grounds.

Baseball & Celebrities

Six-time Grammy winner, co-founder of the Eagles rock band and big baseball fan, Glenn Frey sat next to Vin Scully in the broadcast booth and helped call the June 23, 1985 game between the Dodgers and Astros.

Mailbox money! Slugger Keith Hernandez received $15,000 for appearing on two episodes of the *Jerry Seinfeld* show in 1992 and still gets about $3,000 a year in residuals.

Big time owners! Bing Crosby, Bob Hope and Gene Autry have all owned MLB teams.

Actor Chuck Connors is one of only 12 people to play in both the NBA (Celtics) and MLB (Dodgers/Cubs).

Robert Redford attended the University of Colorado on a baseball scholarship.

Country music star Billy Ray Cyrus won a baseball scholarship to Georgetown College but turned to music after a voice inside his head told him: "Trade in your catcher's mitt and buy a guitar."

A really big show! Television personality Ed Sullivan worked for the New York Graphic as sports editor in the 1920s.

I'd rather be big time! Former CBS News reporter and anchorman Dan Rather got his start in radio calling play-by-play for the minor league Houston Buffs.

> "There's no crying in baseball!"
> – Tom Hanks in *A League of Their Own*

Abstract impressionist artist Elaine de Kooning travelled with MLB teams in the 1950s capturing the players' movements on canvas. Several of her more popular paintings including "Baseball Players," were produced during that time.

Joe DiMaggio, Mickey Mantle and Roy Campanella are all mentioned in Billy Joel's "We Didn't Start the Fire."

In a September 1963 episode of TV's *Mr. Ed*, the affable talking horse decided to try out for the Dodgers. Leo Durocher, Sandy Koufax, Johnny Roseboro and Willie Davis appeared as themselves. SPOILER ALERT: Mr. Ed hits an in-the-park homer off Koufax.

Baseball Hall of Famer Ted Williams is also a member of the Game Fish Hall of Fame in Florida.

Got you covered! A two-and-a-half hour rain delay didn't dampen the spirits in Yankee Stadium on July 25, 2010. It was their annual "Umbrella Day" promotion.

Twice is Nice! Camden Yards in Baltimore has a double-decker bullpen.

Believe It or Not! Baltimore lost their Sunday games 15 weeks in a row in 2008.

Sunday baseball games were banned in the National League until 1892 but it took until 1934 before all teams consented to play on the Sabbath.

Joe Gordon got exactly 1,000 hits in the 1,000 games he played for the New York Yankees.

"Beethoven can't really be great because his picture isn't on a bubble gum card."
– Charles Schulz

Warren Spahn joined MLB at the age of 21 and pitched for 21 seasons, won 21 games eight times and wore uniform number 21.

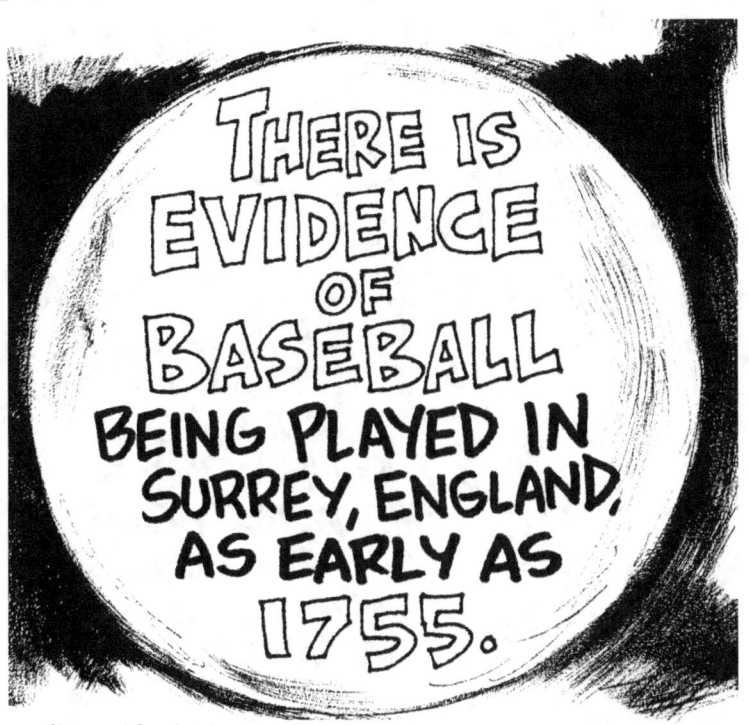

The Tigers and the Pirates played a pair of nine-inning scoreless games in three days in May 2013 – only the fifth time this has happed in more than 100 years of Major League play.

Baker Bowl, home of the Phillies 1887-1938, had a swimming pool under the clubhouse.

Go figure! The Montreal Expos played 22 of their "home games" in a much warmer Puerto Rico in 2003.

Go Philly! In 1980, sports teams from **Philadelphia** contested the Stanley Cup, the NBA Finals, the World Series and Super Bowl XV, winning only the World Series.

Earring Delay! Manny Ramirez lost his $15,000 diamond earring when he slid headfirst into third base. The game was stopped as he crawled around in the dirt hunting for it. His reaction, when he couldn't find it: "Don't worry about it. I've got money. I can buy another one."

The average Major League field has 9,000 square feet of grass.

Ripley's — Believe It or Not!

John Miller had two home runs in his two-year MLB career. The first was his first time at bat for the Yankees in 1966. His second was his last time batting in the MLB for the Dodgers in 1999. In between he had 59 hits.

Nine MLB players have been presented the Presidential Medal of Freedom, the latest being Stan Musial in 2011.

Early Major Leaguers were required to pay 50-cents per game for rooms while on the road.

> "I knew when my career was over. In 1965, my baseball card came out with no picture."
> – Bob Uecker

Bob Feller struck out 17 batters in a single game on September 13, 1936 when he was 17 years old.

Boston's Mike Greenwell hit two homers including a grand slam driving in all nine runs while beating Seattle 9-8 on September 2, 1996.

Corey Stockhouse of Farmington, New Mexico is trying to collect every card made of Tim Wallach, who spent 17 years in the majors. By late 2015, he had collected 15,744 of them. He wants every card ever printed, not just one of each card.

Picky. Picky!
Cleveland was forced to forfeit a game in 1903 when its second baseman Napoleon Lajoie threw a scuffed and discolored ball into the stands.

> "A baseball game is simply a nervous breakdown divided into nine innings."
> – Columnist Earl Wilson

Pitcher Joey Jay was the first Little League player who grew up to play in the Major Leagues.

Jay retired from the big leagues in 1966 following 13 years with a record of 99 wins and 999 strikeouts.

Not a bad start! The Yankees' Russ Van Atta made his MLB debut on April 25, 1933 by throwing a complete game shut-out against the Washington Senators 16-0. He also went 4 for 4 at the plate with a sacrifice, three runs scored and an RBI.

A bloody sock worn by Red Sox pitcher Curt Schilling during the 2004 World Series was sold at auction in February 2013 for $92,613.

By the end of the 2008 season the Cubs and Dodgers had played each other 2,038 times, with each winning 1,012 with 14 ties.

Ripley's —— Believe It or Not!

Baseball Hall-of-Famer **DAVE WINFIELD** was drafted by the NBA's Atlanta Hawks, the NFL's Minnesota Vikings, and MLB's San Diego Padres, which he joined after graduating college in 1973.

Rangers' George "Doc" Medich, a medical student during the off-season, saved the life of a 73-year-old fan who suffered a heart attack on April 11, 1978 while attending the game.

Believe It or Not! Hank Aaron and Babe Ruth scored the same number of runs in their careers - 2,174.

33 NAMES OF DIFFERENT BASEBALL PLAYERS IN TERRY CASHMAN'S 1981 HIT SONG, "TALKIN' BASEBALL."

Only one MLB regular season home run has been hit in Hawaii. The Cardinals' Ron Gant hit it against the Padres on April 20, 1997 during a series in Aloha Stadium.

Outfielder Joel Youngblood recorded hits for two different MLB teams in two different cities on the same day – August 4, 1982. In the afternoon he had a hit as a Met against the Cubs in Chicago's Wrigley Field; he was traded after that game and connected again for the Montreal Expos in Philadelphia that night.

Fun Baseball Icons to Visit

A red stadium chair is bolted to the wall in the Mall of America in Bloomington, Minnesota where the iconic Metropolitan Stadium once stood. It marks the spot where the Twins' Harmon Killebrew smacked a 522-foot homer into the second deck seats on June 3, 1967. It was the longest home run ever hit in the park. A plaque in the floor also marks the location of the Metropolitan home plate.

Nearly 5,000 baseballs are in the World's Largest Collection of Autographed Baseballs in the St. Petersburg (Florida) Museum of History. In addition to balls signed by the great players of all times, there are balls autographed by celebrities, ranging from Elvis to Fidel Castro to Amelia Earhart.

Ripley's — Believe It or Not!

It would take a 500-foot homer for the ball to fall into the giant glove in the left field stands of AT&T Park in San Francisco, home of the Giants. The Giant 1927 old-time baseball glove is 27-feet tall by 30-feet wide.

Great for selfies! Statues of Bart, Lisa, Marge and Homer Simpson can be found in the stadium of the Albuquerque Isotopes minor league team, which took its name from the fictitious Springfield Isotopes in the TV show, *The Simpsons*.

Visit the grave of Ray Chapman, the only player to be killed by a baseball during a MLB game. A sign in front of his modest headstone in Lake View Cemetery in Cleveland Heights, Ohio, notes that "Baseball fans paid for this monument with nickels and dimes."

> DURING A MLB® 1988 GAME, ASTROS PITCHER **JIM DESHAIES** ATTEMPTED TO USE WITCHCRAFT TO BREAK HIS TEAM'S LOSING STREAK — AND THEY BEAT THE PADRES 4 TO 1!

Lucky catcher. Jeff Torborg was behind the plate for two no-hitters: Sandy Koufax on September 9, 1965 and Nolan Ryan on May 5, 1973.

Superstitious? Pitcher Rube Waddell was born on Friday, October 13, 1876 and died on April Fool's Day 1914. He played 13 years in the big leagues.

During his 19-year MLB career Willie Wilson hit 13 inside-the-park home runs, the most of any Major Leaguer playing after 1950.

The Cardinals defeated the Tigers in the 1934 World Series in four games with Jerome "Dizzy" Dean and his kid brother Paul "Daffy" Dean each winning two games, accounting for all four Cardinal victories.

Another set of brothers, William and Gene Hargrave had the not-so-macho nicknames of Pinky and Bubbles.

Girls were officially allowed to play in Little League games starting on June 12, 1974.

HIGH-VELOCITY PITCHERS!

The 2015 World Series matchup was a showcase for the fastest throwers in MLB. During the season, 14.8% of all pitches thrown by the Royals were clocked at more than 95 mph; the Mets pitched 95 mph or more 22.1% of the time.

Hall of Fame pitcher Hoyt Wilhelm had 493 plate appearances in his 21-year career and hit only one home run – his very first at bat as a New York Giant on April 23, 1952.

Believe it or Not! Hall Of Famer Tony Gwynn got his first Major League hit on July 19, 1982. Exactly 24 years later on July 19, 2006, Tony Gwynn Jr. connected on his first hit in the Major Leagues.

Yankees owner George Steinbrenner was banned from baseball twice: In 1974 for making illegal campaign contributions and again in 1990 for hiring a private investigator to spy on his players. He was re-instated both times.

2015 ATTENDANCE
at 30 MLB Stadiums

Total MLB attendance for the 2,429 regular season games was 73,760,020, up 162,221 over 2014.

Los Angeles Dodgers led all home parks with 3,764,815 for an average of 46,479.

Tampa Bay Rays hosted the least number of fans with 1,247,668 for an average of 15,403.

World Series teams. Royals greeted 2,708,549 fans, with an average of 33,438; the Mets, 2,569,753, with an average of 31,725.

The Orioles beat the White Sox 8-2 on April 29, 2015 in front of **46,000 EMPTY SEATS**. The game was closed to the public due to the unrest and rioting taking place that week in Baltimore.

Ripley's—Believe It or Not!

Nice streak! Eric Hinske played in three consecutive World Series with three different teams: the Boston Red Sox (2007), The Tampa Bay Rays (2008); and the New York Yankees (2009).

The Pirates' error-prone Dick "Dr. Strangeglove" Stuart recalls: "One night in Pittsburgh, 30,000 fans gave me a standing ovation for catching a hotdog wrapper on the fly."

When asked in 1930 how he felt about holding out for a salary larger than President Herbert Hoover's, Babe Ruth quickly replied, "Why not, I had a better year than he did."

> "You don't realize how easy this game is until you get up in that broadcasting booth."
> – Mickey Mantle

The ball that Cardinals' Mark McGwire hit over the fence for his 70th and final home run in his record setting 1998 season was sold at auction on January 12, 1999 for $3,054,000.

The WAVE, now popular in virtually all stadiums and all sports was "invented" by baseball fan Krazy George Henderson during a game between the Yankees and the A's at the Oakland Coliseum on October 15, 1981.

IN 1938 **HENRY HELF** OF THE CLEVELAND INDIANS CAUGHT A BASEBALL THAT WAS DROPPED 708 FEET — AND THOUGHT TO BE TRAVELING AT 138 MPH — FROM THE TOP OF CLEVELAND'S TERMINAL TOWER.

The Cleveland Indians won 17 consecutive extra-inning games and went 20-3 in extended games during the 1949 season.

Long and tall of the game. The shortest MLB player was Eddie Gaedel, who was three feet, seven inches tall. He batted once for the St. Louis Browns as a publicity stunt. The tallest player in MLB history is pitcher Jon Rauch, who spent 11 years in the majors, at six feet, eleven inches tall.

No need to change perfection!
The official weight and size of a Major League baseball have not been altered since 1872, when the standards were set.

There was a hump in center field of Baker Bowl, home of the Phillies, over a subway tunnel that ran under the park. Players could feel the ground shake as a train passed.

"Not true at all. Vaseline is manufactured right here in the United States."
– Don Sutton, when accused of using foreign substances on his pitches.

Baseball is the only team sport where the playing field has different dimensions, as nearly all 30 MLB ballparks have different outfield dimensions and configurations.

A person must be a high school graduate to play ball in the big leagues.

The New York Mets were named after The Metropolitans, a 19th century baseball club that had played in New York.

ALL GAMES OF THE 1944 WORLD SERIES BETWEEN THE ST. LOUIS BROWNS AND THE ST. LOUIS CARDINALS WERE PLAYED IN THE SAME STADIUM — SPORTSMAN'S PARK, BECAUSE IT WAS THE HOME FIELD TO *BOTH TEAMS.*

No one born in Cooperstown, New York, the home of the Baseball Hall of Fame, has ever played Major League baseball.

Rollie Fingers' iconic handlebar mustache was the result of an offer that A's owner Charlie Finley presented to his players. He wanted his men to grow facial hair before a planned Father's Day promotion. Fingers grew the best and won $300 and a $100 jar of mustache wax.

> "Lady, I'm not an athlete. I'm a professional baseball player."
> – John Kruk

Casey Stengel was 70 when the Yankees fired him after losing the 1960 World Series. "I'll never make the mistake of being 70 again," he later told reporters.

Omar Olivares wore his initials, "00" as his number during his time with both the Cardinals in 1993 and the Phillies in 1995.

Since 1938 most balls used in MLB games are rubbed in Lena Blackburne Baseball Rubbing Mud to dull the sheen that comes on the new ball. The unique mud can only be found in a secret location near Palmyra, New Jersey.

GAME SEVEN OF THE 1960 WORLD SERIES IS THE ONLY WORLD SERIES GAME IN HISTORY NOT TO HAVE A STRIKEOUT THE ENTIRE GAME.

Ripley's—— Believe It or Not!

Look out! The Cardinals' Vince Coleman missed the 1985 World Series due to an injury he received when he was partially rolled up in a tarp. It started raining, the tarpaulin machine was rolled out and Coleman saw it too late.

1948 – The last year the Chicago White Sox wore solid white socks.

The Pirates' Willie Stargell was the first player to hit the ball completely out of Dodger Stadium on August 5, 1969 with a 507 foot homer. He did it again in 1973 with a 470 foot wallop.

21 HITS ON OCTOBER 12, 2015, THE MOST EVER IN A SINGLE GAME OF POST-SEASON PLAY — CARDINALS VS. THE CUBS.

Japanese swordsman **Isao Machii** can slice a fastball in two that's pitched to him at 100 mph!

Ripley's — Believe It or Not!

The Texas Rangers lost the use of Elvis Andrus for two days during spring 2013 – due to the inflammation of a new tattoo.

To get even with an unpopular umpire, Mudcat Grant, a pitcher for the Cleveland Indians, secured horse manure to the back of catcher Joe Ascue's helmet. As the umpire bent over to call the game, he got a huge whiff and backed up further and further as the game proceeded. Grant said it was the quickest game he ever pitched.

With a runner on third base, catcher Dave Bresnahan of the Williamsport (Pennsylvania) Bills threw a potato carved to look like a ball wildly at his third baseman, making it look like a sloppy attempt at a pickoff. The runner ran home, only to be tagged out by the catcher holding the real ball. The potato was retrieved, the runner was safe, Bresnahan was kicked out and released the next day.

> "I say this from the bottom of my heart, that if you don't root for the Dodgers, you might not get to heaven."
> – Tommy Lasorda

The right field wall in Pittsburgh's PNC Park is 21 feet tall, honoring the Pirate's revered right fielder, #21 Roberto Clemente.

REAL LIFE Baseball Humor
ALL THESE STORIES ALLEGEDLY HAPPENED

A rookie sat next to his manager and watched Roger Maris gun down a runner trying to go from first to third.

"Kid, you won't see a throw like that again in a million years."

Three innings later, Maris did it again.

The rookie turned to the manager and said, "Time sure flies up here in the majors."

"I'll never forget September 6, 1950. I got a letter threatening me, Hank Bauer, Yogi Berra and Johnny Mize. It said if I showed up in uniform against the Red Sox I'd be shot. I turned the letter over to the FBI and told my manager Casey Stengel about it. You know what Casey did? He gave me a different uniform and gave mine to Billy Martin. Can you imagine that! Guess Casey thought it'd be better if Billy got shot."
– Phil Rizzuto

Before the 1952 World Series, Brooklyn Dodgers' manager Charlie Dressen cornered pitcher Billy Loes.

"I see in the paper where you picked the Yankees to beat us in seven games. What's wrong with you," Dressen said.

"I was misquoted," Loes protested. "I picked them in six games."

Ripley's — Believe It or Not!

In 1934, Brooklyn Dodger manager Casey Stengel went out to the mound to remove his battered pitcher, Walter "Boom-Boom" Beck. Boom-Boom was not happy and in a fit of temper turned around and threw the ball high and hard toward the right-field wall. Dodger right fielder Hack Wilson, who had not been paying attention to what was going on in the infield, heard the ball hit the wall behind him. He saw it, quickly ran over and threw it to second base before he fully realized how the ball got out to him in the first place.

On a windy day in San Francisco, third baseman Rocky Bridges called for a popup. He drifted past the shortstop, past the pitcher on the mound, past the second baseman. Finally, he was standing next to first baseman Vic Power as the ball fell four feet behind them.

The next day, the newspaper ran a string of song parodies, one targeting Bridges:

"A tisket, a tasket. I should have brought a basket."

Bridges awaited the writer in the clubhouse the following day. "Hey you, c'mon over here. I read what you wrote in the paper."

"And?"

"And it bothered me so much I couldn't sleep last night. I've got to ask you... How does the tune to that song go?"

Asked the age of his two elderly pinch-hitters – Vic Davalillo and Manny Mota – Los Angeles manager Tommy Lasorda shrugged.

"I don't know but somebody told me they were waiters at the last supper."

Tim O'Brien is writer/photographer and chief wordsmith with Casa Flamingo Literary Arts, a boutique publishing house in Nashville, Tennessee. He has spent more than 40 years chronicling a diverse range of outdoor entertainment industries from amusement parks and carnivals to sideshows and baseball stadiums. He served as VP Publishing & Communications for Ripley Entertainment Inc. from 2004 through 2014 and 18 years as senior editor of *Amusement Business*, the world's leading business magazine for the amusement park and attraction industries. During his colorful career, the award winning photojournalist has published more than 10,000 articles and 6,000 photos and has had 16 books published. His most recent books, all biographies, are *Ward Hall – King of the Sideshow; Tony Baxter – First of the Second Generation of Walt Disney Imagineers;* and *Dick Kinzel – Roller Coaster King of Cedar Point Amusement Park.*

John Graziano is only the 7th person to take up the pen illustrating the Ripley's syndicated daily cartoon originated by Robert Ripley in 1918. John has been working as an artist and illustrator since 1983, when he received a certificate in illustration from the Newark School of Fine and Industrial Arts. John later studied Industrial Design Technology at the Art Institute of Pittsburgh. He has designed trading card sets and a portrait series based on the 1960s cult TV show *Dark Shadows*. John has also created comic strips for *Scream Queens* magazine, sculpted figures that have been made into wax museum pieces, provided book illustrations, plastic model kit box illustrations, designed t-shirt graphics and created storyboards and concept drawings for Hollywood films. Recently John worked on a series of fun books for Ripley publishing which included an 8-book series titled "Shout Outs!" and provided illustrations for the latest Ripley "Twist" book on Pirates. John is also a musician and plays bass, guitar and sings with the band "Feeling Groovy," performing the feel-good pop/rock of the 60s, 70s, 80s and beyond!